OXFORD

Secular

BC243

SA (with divisions) and piano

RED BOOTS ON

Red Boots On

Kit Wright (b. 1944)

BOB CHILCOTT

Duration: 2 mins

If performing in two parts, sing the first and second soprano lines in bars 19–22 and 37–44, and the second soprano and second alto lines in bar 48–51.

win-ter-time. She's got Red boots on, she's got

Red boots on, Kick-ing up the win-ter Till the win-ter's gone.

Red boots on, she's got Red boots on,— she's got Red boots on.—

_____ Red boots on, Oh Red boots on.—

tin-gle in her toes And new red boots on Wher-ev-er she goes.

She's got Red boots on,_____ she's got Red boots on,

Red boots on, she's got Red boots on,_ she's got Red boots on._____ Red boots on,

she's got Red boots on._____ Red boots on,

Oh Red boots on._____

All a-round Lake Street, Up by St Paul, Quick-er than the white wind

Love takes all: Ma-ry Lou's walk-ing In the big snow fall.

S. She's got Red boots on, she's got Red boots on,

A.1 She's got Red boots on, she's got Red boots on,

A.2 She's got She's got Red boots on,

Bob Chilcott has been involved with choral music all his life, first as a Chorister and then a Choral Scholar at King's College, Cambridge. Later, he sang and composed music for 12 years with the King's Singers. His experiences with that group, his passionate commitment to young and amateur choirs, and his profound belief that music can unite people, have inspired him both to compose full-time and, through proactive workshopping, to promote choral music worldwide.

Have you tried?

The angel Gabriel (ISBN 978–0–19–343325–0)
The Marvellous Birth (ISBN 978–0–19–335898–0)
Mid-winter (ISBN 978–0–19–341523–2)
The Three Kings (ISBN 978–0–19–340061–0)

For more details about Bob Chilcott and his music, please contact Oxford University Press, Music Department.

OXFORD
UNIVERSITY PRESS

www.oup.com

ISBN 978-0-19-336511-7

9 780193 365117